THE
DUTY OF
PROCREATION

DAVID DAUBE

TO MY
THREE
SONS

6

THE
DUTY OF
PROCREATION

DAVID DAUBE

EDINBURGH
at the University Press

6

©

David Daube 1977
EDINBURGH UNIVERSITY PRESS
22 George Square, Edinburgh

ISBN 0 85224 330 8

Printed in Great Britain
by W. & J. Mackay Limited
Chatham

Preface

ᘐ

This essay is the Presidential Address to the Classical Association, delivered at Liverpool on 14 April 1977, on the occasion of the Annual General Meeting.

I have taken the opportunity presented by publication – for which I am grateful to Edinburgh University Press – to include the appropriate apparatus of footnotes and references that oral presentation excludes, in the hope that the usefulness of this short work will be enhanced thereby.

DAVID DAUBE
School of Law
University of California
Berkeley

Contents

❧

❧

The Duty of Procreation

6

The duty to procreate is central in traditional Jewish and Christian life. It is true that Christianity in principle prefers celibacy. But if you are not up to it – and the vast majority of humans are not – the proper path to take is the Jewish one: marriage with a view to having children. The dutiful seeking of children will justify the non-celibate, second-best course.

In today's address it will be contended that the duty came into these religions from heathen politics. The argument will proceed in three parts: the first will be devoted to the lack of Biblical authority, the second to the development of the duty in classical antiquity, and the third to its reception by Rabbis and Church Fathers.

1) *The Bible* (

WITH THE POSSIBLE exception of two to three verses in the Pastoral Epistles, Scripture contains no trace of the duty; nor, it may be observed, is it evidenced anywhere in the ancient Near East. To be sure, both in the Old Testament and in the New, children are a boon, childlessness is a misfortune: the Lucan Elisabeth, pregnant after many years of barrenness, expresses her relief in the same words as Rachel in Genesis.[1] But this implies no obligation. Biblical writers find it great to have an ample supply of wine, sound hearing and regular teeth (well, a woman at least would be admired for them) and rough to reside in an area struck by famine.[2] It does not follow that you ought to keep a cellar, visit the ear specialist and dentist or move to where there is enough to eat. Normally, you will in fact do your best towards those desirable ends, including procreation – which, however, is very different from having to act. If you do not, that is your choice; you are committing no wrong whatsoever.

The exponents of the orthodox doctrine could not, of course, admit this: they need a Scriptural basis, so they do invoke a number of passages. However, these are not only pitifully few, considering the enormous importance of the matter, but also, if looked at with detachment, far from providing the requisite support. Yet many modern scholars still follow the customary, time-hallowed line.

The two principal texts both come from Genesis.

[1] Luke 1.25, Genesis 30.23.
[2] 'Wine' Genesis 27.28, John 2.3ff.; 'hearing' II Samuel 19.36; 'teeth' Song of Solomon 4.2, 6.6; 'famine' Genesis 41ff., I Kings 18.2ff., Ruth 1.

One is God's pronouncement – uttered four times, once to Adam and Eve on the Friday of the creation, twice to Noah and his sons after the flood and once to Jacob – 'be fruitful and multiply'. The other is the story of Onan.[1] However, as for the former, it is not a commandment but a blessing. (Though one of Chaucer's ladies treats it as both.[2]) This is evident from the form employed in the Hebrew[3] as well as from the continuation as it appears the first time: 'and have dominion over the fish of the sea and over the fowl of the air' – never promoted to a *mizwah*. Moreover, on two occasions it is expressly introduced by 'and God blessed them'. Above all, the identical phrase is addressed on the fifth day of the creation to fish and fowl,[4] obviously not intended to become responsible for their reproduction. Here, too, not surprisingly, we read 'and God blessed them'. It is a blessing, nothing else.

The new *Encyclopedia Judaica*[5] still calls it 'a commandment'. The *Dictionnaire de Théologie Catholique*,[6] while formulating more correctly, manages to achieve much the same effect. It does avoid the label 'com-

---

[1] Genesis 1.28, 9.1, 7, 35.11, 38.6ff. For a typical coupling of the two, see F.R. Walton, *Diodorus of Sicily* (Loeb Classical Library) vol.12 (1967) p.285.

[2] 'God bad us' and 'this gentil text': G. Chaucer, *Canterbury Tales*, The Wife of Bath's Prologue 28f.

[3] cp. Exodus 4.18, Deuteronomy 33.18.   [4] Genesis 1.22.

[5] Art. 'Children' by Editorial Staff, vol.5 (1971) p.426.

[6] Art. 'Mariage' by L. Godefrey, vol.9:2 (1927) p.2045.

mandment' and begins by stating that God, having created life, *bénit*, 'blesses', it. But then it goes on to speak of a *mot d'ordre*, 'watchword', to our first parents. This comes close enough to 'commandment' for the ordinary reader at least to conclude that that is what we have to do with. An eminently subtle presentation.

Onan, the Bible tells us, 'spilled (his semen) on the ground' and was slain by God. This incident has played a fateful role in the putting down of sex. For it has been seen as doing far more than inculcate the duty to procreate: namely, as utterly condemning any use of semen other than for the purpose of pro-creation. Contraception and masturbation provoke the wrath of heaven.

But all this rests on a misunderstanding.[1] The story presupposes neither a general obligation to leave children nor a general prohibition of waste of seed. If we read it without giving way to wishful thinking, Onan was punished for treachery to his deceased brother, for selfishly putting material gain above family loyalty. His elder brother had been given a wife by their father but had died before having progeny. In accordance with the custom of time, the father now bade Onan take over the widow: their first child would then count as his elder brother's and preserve the latter's name. That, of course, would

[1] See D. Daube, *Juridical Review* 62 (1950) pp.71ff.; J. T. Noonan *Contraception* (1965) pp.34ff., 52ff.

mean a substantial diminution of Onan's prospects –
this child, representing his dead brother, would be
entitled to a share in the inheritance (in fact, a major
one if a rule like that in Deuteronomy, favouring the
elder,[1] was already operating). He decided to avert
such loss and, while formally complying with his
father's orders, resorted to *coitus interruptus*. Remember that if he married other wives in addition,
the children would be his own, not encroaching on
what his father would leave. It was only the first child
from the widow that would replace the deceased and
thus do him out of a share. With her, therefore, 'he
spilled to the ground', and it was this base betrayal
that was hateful to God.

It emerges that the legend – just like the Deutero-
nomic law dealing with the refusal to enter into a
levirate union[2] – does bring out an exceptional situation where you must do your best to produce offspring: where it is not for yourself but in your
deceased brother's behalf. It is a blessing to have one's
name carried on by subsequent generations and,
given certain conditions, a surviving brother is to
help the dead one to enjoy it. To infer from this a
basic obligation to procreate is fallacious. Had Onan
begotten a child for the deceased and then practised
coitus interruptus, with the widow and ten more
women, forgoing the perpetuation of his own name,

[1] Deuteronomy 21.15ff.   [2] Deuteronomy 25.5ff.

he would have incurred no reproach. There is nothing strange in this. It is in the very nature of a boon that, while as far as your own person is concerned, you are free to take it or leave it, you must not withhold it from others. A sufficiency of food or a donkey in good shape is a pleasant thing to have. Yet there is no injunction in the Bible against starving myself should I be so minded or against saying good riddance if my own ass break down; indeed I may shoot it even when it is in perfect condition and sell its hide or make a bonfire with it. But – note the analogy to Onan's case – Biblical law does call on me to allow a corner of my field to be harvested by the poor and to help up another man's ass that has fallen.[1] (It would be very wrong of you to withhold support from your son studying law at Boalt Hall. This implies not the slightest reflection on a person who elects to pass up that opportunity.)

It need hardly be added that the idea of reproving waste of seed as such is quite foreign to this narrative. Actually, it is met nowhere in Scripture; not one of the catalogues of vices in Old Testament wisdom preaching or New Testament denunciations of Pharisees or heathens alludes to it. Yet language has forever misbranded the culprit. He perpetrated treachery to his deceased brother; later interpreters saw his lapse in the *coitus interruptus*, the waste of seed, as such; the

[1] Leviticus 19.9f., Exodus 22.5.

most glaring variety of waste of seed is masturbation; so, from the eighteenth century, masturbation is called onanism.

We come to a third passage occasionally adduced, from the Book of Tobit, around 200 B.C.[1] Even if it did make reproduction obligatory, it would be poor evidence since the work is not free from Greek features. But it does not.

The young heroine of the tale is given by her father to one husband after another, seven altogether. None of them has a right to her, so a demon murders them all before they can consummate the marriage. At last Tobias appears on the scene. He is her nearest kinsman and has been advised that they are preordained for one another.[2] In the wedding-night he exorcises the demon and prays to God: 'And now I take not this my sister from lust but in truth'. Almost certainly, he means that he is acting from allegiance to his family and people: that sets him apart from his predecessors.[3] Hebrew *be'emeth* or an Aramaic equivalent, which may lurk behind 'in truth', would be very suitable for expressing this thought. From the context, it is just conceivable that he is speaking of himself as joining up with a helpmeet, in compliance with God's design when supplementing the male by the

[1] Tobit 8.7.
[2] cp. *Tosephta Qiddushin* 1.4, *Babylonian Sanhedrin* 76b.
[3] cp. *Babylonian Yebamoth* 39b; see F. Zimmermann, *The Book of Tobit* (1958) pp.94f.

female.[1] What is utterly unacceptable is the Vulgate's rendering: 'solely from delight in descendants, among whom your name may be blessed in all eternity.'[2] No reader not brought up in the Church could possibly spot in the term 'in truth' a theme taken up nowhere else. And how elaborately it is developed: Tobias marries from the approved motive, 'delight in descendants'; it is his only one – 'solely from delight in descendants'; and the purpose of progeny is one which, we shall see, derives from Plato, the ensuring of continued worship of God, 'among whom your name may be blessed in all eternity'. In a way, this treatment of the text underlines the absence of true Scriptural support for the duty to procreate: to put so heavy a gloss on a simple phrase is desperation. Cicero, incidentally, charges a man with marrying not from lust but from a worse motive.[3]

The Book of Tobit, like the rest of the Bible, does place the highest value on children: they are a blessing.[4] Wealth is a blessing, too, though of lesser rank.[5] Of a duty to seek either there is no mention.

This leaves the Pastoral Epistles.[6] In 1 Timothy,

[1] Genesis 2.20; see I. Heinemann, *Philons griechische und jüdische Bildung* (1932) pp.270f.
[2] *Non luxuriae causa sed sola posteritatis dilectione in qua benedicatur nomen tuum in saecula saeculorum.*   [3] Cicero, *pro Sestio* 52.110.
[4] Tobit 2.1, 5.16 (15)ff., 8.17, 10.4ff., 11, 11.14ff.
[5] Tobit 1.20, 4.21, 8.21, 11.15.
[6] 1 Timothy 2.15, 5.11ff., Titus 2.5. For alternative interpretations of 1 Timothy 2.15, see C.K.Barrett, *The Pastoral Epistles in the English Bible* (1963) p.56.

women, tainted by Eve's primal sin, may achieve salvation through childbearing; and young widows, in danger of falling into bad ways, had better remarry and bear children. In Titus, the older women are to teach the younger ones to love their husbands and children.

Once again, procreation does not really figure as an ought. After all, sin is expiable through the loss of dear ones or the experiencing of a crippling disease – which implies no obligation to kill those you cherish or to spoon up a bacteria culture. The silence of the Epistles as to any responsibility of men in this connection is highly significant. It would be rash to say more than that, perhaps, the verses in question indicate a trend towards a duty.

2) *The West* (

GREECE. When we now turn to classical antiquity, the overall picture is radically different. The duty to procreate occupies a prominent place, both in its unconditional form preached by Judaism – take a wife and have children – and in its conditional one, characteristic of Christianity – if marry you must, it may be only for the sake of having children. Nevertheless, even in this part of the world, the very earliest layers of civilization accessible to us contain neither variety. Not a single one of the ancient Greek myths hints at a duty, not a single line in Homer; and in the case of so fundamental a concern, the argument from silence cannot be brushed aside.

Actually, in this remote phase, the Greeks were quite afraid of over-population.[1] It comes out in their perennial urge to colonize, due to inadequate living space.[2] Their sagas about the past, too, show it. Cadmus, when he founded Thebes, obtained warriors from a dragon's teeth which he had sown; these fell upon each other and he aided them in their mutual killing till only five survived. It is commonly held that something must have gone wrong with the transmission of the episode: why should Cadmus, wanting residents for his city, abet the slaughter?[3] This is far from absurd, however, if the need for a limited size was felt. Another reminiscence surely archaic is the attribution of the Trojan war to a plan of the gods 'to lighten the earth, oppressed with over-increase of her sons'.[4] (A puzzling clause, incidentally, occurring in Genesis, has a similar ring[5] and suggests that, in the most primitive version of the story of the flood, the latter was sent not as a punishment of wickedness but

[1] See D. Daube, *Medical and Genetic Ethics* (1976) p.12.
[2] See H. Bengtson, *Griechische Geschichte*, 3rd ed. (1965) pp.20f., 46, 56f., 66ff.
[3] See F. Jacoby, in Pauly-Wissowas *Real-Encyclopädie der classischen Altertumswissenschaft*, vol.10:2 (1919) p.1465, referring to P. Friedländer who, however, goes less far: *Rheinisches Museum für Philologie* 69 (1914) pp.309f.
[4] Euripides, *Orestes* 1641f., translation by A.S. Way, *Euripides* (Loeb Classical Library) vol.2 (1924) p.273.
[5] Genesis 6.1.

as a cure of overpopulation: things went downhill, we learn, 'when men began to multiply on the face of the earth'. Also pertinent is the notice that 'the land was not able to bear them – Abram and Lot – that they might live together'.[1]) Hesiod is still extremely reserved as to the number of children that can be afforded.[2]

This does not mean that, precisely in the olden times with conservative values, most couples did not in fact want children. Niobe was proud of having more than Leto and turned into a weeping stone on losing them. But, then, Artemis was no less entitled to her single lifestyle. No doubt, in very special circumstances, you might be pressured into parenthood; say you came from a particularly respected royal line, which your subjects felt should continue.[3] Such cases stand out against a background of absolute freedom in this sphere.

The fundamental change occurred around 500 B.C., under the impact of the threat from Persia, 'populous Asia', 'a mighty flood of men', in Aeschylus's words.[4] Herodotus relates that the army of Xerxes consisted of 1,700,000 infantry and 80,000 cavalry.[5] It may be exaggerated,[6] but it shows how the defenders viewed their situation. From those days, though many

[1] Genesis 13.6.   [2] Hesiod, *Works and Days* 376ff.
[3] Herodotus, *History* 5.39ff.   [4] Aeschylus, *Persians* 73, 83.
[5] Herodotus, *History* 7.60, 87.
[6] See H. Bengtson, op. cit., pp.163f.

thinkers prescribed abstention – men all of them, and chiefly speaking to men, who would be deflected from higher things by women's inferior charms – official policy was in favour of fertility. Had the people been universally *kinderfreudig*, keen on offspring, coercion would not have been called for; but the culture was already urbanized enough to cause widespread reluctance to marry or complicate marriage by progeny. Legal and ethical norms, therefore, came into being, requiring that you marry and have children or at least – this would be a compromise with the celibacy-school – that, if you marry, you do so in order to have children and not from frivolity.

Several factors contributed to this movement, one of them the competition between the individual Greek communities whose internecine wars decimated their youth. Thucydides, while fully aware how easily a city might become too large to feed its inhabitants, also notices its helplessness vis-à-vis a more numerous rival.[1] 'Where are the sons that we sent to the battlefields?', mourns Aristophanes's Lysistrata, and peace, he hopes, will not only repair the devastated lands but also make good the losses in men.[2] We must bear in mind, further, that in many a city – Sparta, for example – those free dreaded being

[1] Thucydides, *History of the Peloponnesian War* 1.2.
[2] Aristophanes, *Lysistrata* 589f. – translation by B.B. Rogers, *Aristophanes* (Loeb Classical Library) vol.3 (1946) p.61 – *The Peace* 1320f.

swamped by their slaves and serfs. Again, in the vast royal realms forming on the death of Alexander, there was much territory waiting to be settled.[1] No need here to go into the relative weight of these and other pressures, greatly varying, of course, from one time or place to another.

Sparta imposed on bachelors both a measure of civic disgrace and a fine.[2] Plato's *Laws* do the same.[3] At Sparta, too, a father of three sons was exempt from the army, one of four from other dues as well.[4] Athens went less far: a childless man was excluded from high office.[5] Aristophanes, in the *Symposium*, at first sight appears to quote a regulation which, like the Spartan one, makes it incumbent on all men to procreate.[6] However, apart from the possibility of interpolation, the passage can be understood in a different sense.

Spinsters were not penalized. Presumably, the assumption was that a woman would remain single only if no man would have her.[7] Still, in Plato's *Republic*, where he offers a more basic analysis of

---

[1] See H. Bengtson, op. cit., pp.114, 408, 421.

[2] Stobaeus, *Anthology* 67.16; Plutarch, *Lysander* 30.5, *Lycurgus* 15.1f., *Sayings of Spartans*, Lycurgus 14 (*Moralia* 227F); Athenaeus, *Deipnosophists* 13.555C.

[3] Plato, *Laws* 4.11.721, 6.17.774; see J. H. Lipsius, *Attisches Recht und Rechtsverfahren*, vol.2, pt.1 (1908) p.341.

[4] Aristotle, *Politics* 2.6.13.1270b.

[5] Dinarchus, *Against Demosthenes* 99.71.

[6] Plato, *Symposium* 16.192B; see J. H. Lipsius, op. cit., p.342.

[7] cp. Athenaeus, *Deipnosophists*, l.c.

marriage, women as well as men are spoken of as under a duty to procreate 'for the state'.[1]

Plato, indeed, like Thucydides, realizes that though numbers are needed for defence, a population should fit its territory. So he makes provision against what he deems excessive increase. Moreover, fundamentally contemptuous of the flesh, he denounces all sexual commerce save that with your wife for the purpose of procreation.[2] As usual, he endows his policy with an idealistic aura: reproduction is humanity's way of partaking in immortality and it ensures a continuous stream of worshippers of God.[3] Even quite recent exposés devote exclusive attention to 'the moral beauty of this conception'.[4] But while there is definitely room for such a mode of appreciation, the picture is most incomplete if we overlook the regime's desire for soldiers, cannon fodder.

Aristotle's discussion in his *Politics* is modelled on the *Republic*.[5] He details the correct ages for marriage and procreation with respect to both men and women, without mentioning any sanctions in the event of disobedience. This does not prove that he has none in mind. A man who produces children is said 'to perform

---

[1] Plato, *Republic* 5.9.460E; cp. also *Laws* 11.930C.
[2] Plato, *Laws* 5.737D, 740f., 8.835ff.
[3] Plato, *Laws* 4.721B, 6.773Ef., 776B.
[4] G.R.Morrow, *Plato's Cretan City* (1960) pp.439f., referring to L.R.Farnell, *Higher Aspects of Greek Religion* (1912) p.37.
[5] Aristotle, *Politics* 7.14.1334bff.

a public service' – which echoes 'for the state' in the *Republic* and smacks of a moral duty rather than a legal one. On the other hand, he does advise the law-giver to see to it that a pregnant woman has adequate daily exercise.

We may dispense with a step-by-step examination of Plato's treatment by successive generations. It suffices to note that, as the various schools – the Stoics, above all – were spreading throughout the Mediterranean world, his opinions gained an even wider audience. That, at times, they suffered con- siderable modification goes without saying.

A word of warning, however, may be in place. Not every description in a Greek source of marriage as aiming at procreation presupposes a duty, let alone the tenet that marriage is justifiable only on that ground. The yearning met in Scripture for self- perpetuation in progeny, fully legitimate progeny by preference, is a very general one and, in historical times, marriage is the commonest way everywhere to attain this blessing. King Krt of Ugarit is by no means blind to the charms of the lady he woos, yet his chief consideration is: 'For in my dream Il has granted that a scion be born unto Krt'.[1] This is not in pursuance of any precept, legal or moral; nor does it imply that, save where it serves procreation, intercourse is sinful. The same is true of the Egyptian sage's advice to be

[1] See A. van Selms, *Marriage and Family Life in Ugaritic Literature* (1954) pp.13ff., 40f., 83.

good to your wife, 'a profitable field'.[1] Or of Napoleon marrying Marie-Louise in the hope of securing a worthy successor. Or of the familiar character who, after prolonged and wild bachelorhood, settles down to found a household.

In Greece, too, just as in Israel, normally the hope was for a marriage to be fertile. That goes for husband and wife – remember Niobe – although in both cultures, as a rule, the former would be particularly keen on an heir. The Euripidean Andromache, reduced to slavery, hankers after her past as Hector's 'childbearing spouse'.[2] Designations of this type may date from long before the Persian wars. So may the betrothal 'I give you my daughter for the cultivation (literally, ploughing) of legitimate children'.[3] From Clement of Alexandria on, Church Fathers invoke it as reflecting the regular function of marriage;[4] and insofar as they refrain from admixing Christian ideas, they are correct.

Again, when Xenophon says that men marry not from lust – for this, prostitutes would do – but from a desire for fine children, he need not be thinking on Platonic lines. Neither need Demosthenes, who substitutes a subtler, three-fold division: wives give their

[1] See J. A. Wilson in J. B. Pritchard, *Ancient Near Eastern Texts Relating to the Old Testament* (1950) p.413.
[2] Euripides, *Andromache* 4; see P. T. Stevens, *Euripides, Andromache* (1971) p.88.
[3] Menander, *Fragment* 720.
[4] Clement of Alexandria, *Stromata* 2.23.188.

men legitimate children and guard their households, concubines see to their well-being and mistresses to their enjoyment.[1] Such observations would be possible in many other civilizations.

Lastly, Athenian law allowed you to slay not only him whom you surprised in intercourse with your wife but also him whom you surprised with your concubine kept 'to obtain free (though not fully legitimate) children'.[2] This intent marks off the set-up from a non-committal affair, where you would not be entitled to so extreme a reaction: for one thing, there would not be the risk of having a bastard foisted on you. Even in this statute, it is far from certain that the duty complex plays a part. One can imagine, however, that protection of second-class unions, if they are serious, is found specially urgent in a period when the birthrate is to be boosted and the citizen is encouraged to feel some moral obligation in this respect.

It is not proposed to investigate the bearing, either in Greece or at Rome, of the various attitudes to reproduction on those to exposition of children and infanticide. Little modern work has been done on the

[1] Xenophon, *Memorabilia* 2.2.4, Demosthenes, *Against Neaera* 122.1386.

[2] Demosthenes, *Against Aristocrates* 53.637. J. H. Vince, *Demosthenes* (Loeb Classical Library) vol.3 (1935) p.249, translates *eleutheros* by 'legitimate'. But it should be left its ordinary meaning 'free': the difference between it and *gnesios*, 'legitimate', used in betrothal, is significant. See J. W. Jones, *The Law and Legal Theory of the Greeks* (1956) pp.187, 296.

latter. Their inclusion, therefore, would take up a disproportionate amount of space. It must be left to a future, fuller discussion.

R O M E. The Roman development started when the two censors of 403 B.C. exacted considerable sums from bachelors who had passed the procreative age.[1] The contribution was dubbed *uxorium*, presumably with a touch of sarcasm.[2] Plutarch expressly represents it as necessitated by the losses incurred in war. These would naturally concern the officers whose job it was to count the people; and as the same officers were empowered to promulgate civic guidelines, effective intervention was feasible.

Doubtless the innovating pair borrowed from Greece. Of one of them we know that he had connections with Delphi.[3] Valerius Maximus outlines the speech by which they rebutted protests. It has a Roman-legalistic flavour but, basically, is high-falutin Greek philosophy: your parents, by rearing you, placed you under a debt and if you have evaded repayment for years, you ought in all decency to make up for it.[4]

[1] Valerius Maximus, *Memorable Deeds and Sayings* 2.9.1, Plutarch, *Camillus* 2.2; cp. Plato, *Republic* 5.9.460E, Aristotle, *Politics* 7.14.3.1335a.
[2] Festus, *On the Meaning of Words* (Pauli Excerpta) 379.
[3] See H. W. Parke and D. E. Wormell, *The Delphic Oracle* (1956) vol.1, pp.267ff., vol.2, pp.179f.
[4] cp. Plato, *Laws* 4.717Bf., 721D.

The measure seems to have been temporary only. A more lasting censorian custom was at the five-yearly drawing up of the register to expect a married man to affirm that 'he had a wife in order to seek children'.[1] The expression probably originated in betrothal or wedding, with no thought of duty – maybe in imitation of the Greek 'I give you my daughter for the cultivation of legitimate children'. It brought out the recognized character of the union, and often it would imply a hope or good wish. Even when first incorporated in the censorian lists, it need have meant no more. A Roman marriage could be contracted informally, so might not always look very different from a liaison. Hence, a citizen's assurance that he lived in a proper marriage would make sense.

However, if such was its initial role, it did not last: before long, it was interpreted as indeed referring to a duty. In all likelihood, it did so from the moment it figured in the census. Actually, it may have been introduced along with the bachelor's impost just adverted to, in order to prevent circumvention by a marriage intended to remain sterile.

At this juncture, the divorce of Spurius Carvilius Ruga calls for comment.[2] Valerius Maximus and

[1] Gellius, *Attic Nights* 4.3.2 *liberorum quaerendorum gratia*, 17.21.44 *liberum quaerendorum causa*; Dionysius of Halicarnassus, *Roman Antiquities* 2.25.7 'for the sake of children', *teknon heneka*.

[2] cp. A. Watson, *Tijdschrift Voor Rechtsgeschiedenis* 33 (1965) pp. 38ff.

Plutarch report simply that he divorced his wife because she was barren.[1] Once again, such a step need have nothing to do with a duty of procreation and disapproval of a marriage not geared towards it. In a monogamous society, it would be the plausible solution if a man badly wanted legitimate issue. However, according to Dionysius of Halicarnassus and Aulus Gellius, barrenness would not by itself have led to divorce.[2] What troubled the husband was that he could no longer truthfully swear that he had a wife 'in order to seek children': the declarations at the census were mostly made under oath.[3] To go by this account, he did believe that those words laid a duty on him. Gellius adds that his conduct was most self-denying: he loved her dearly. And he gives two further details underlining the correctness of the proceeding. Their childlessness was due to a physical defect of hers; and he took action only after the traditional consultation with a council of peers.[4]

Which of the two versions is the older? Probably the more elaborate one. Dionysius and Gellius in

[1] Valerius Maximus, *Memorable Deeds and Sayings* 2.1.4; Plutarch, *Comparison of Theseus and Romulus* 6.3, *Comparison of Lycurgus and Numa* 3.6, *Roman Questions* 14, 59 (*Moralia* 267C, 278D).
[2] Dionysius of Halicarnassus, *Roman Antiquities* 2.25.7; Gellius, *Attic Nights* 4.3.2, 17.21.44.
[3] See T. Mommsen, *Römisches Staatsrecht*, vol.2, pt.1, 3rd ed. (1887) pp.362, 373.
[4] cp. Valerius Maximus, *Memorable Deeds and Sayings* 2.9.2.

general draw on good sources. Moreover, whereas it is easy to see how, in popular collections, what was considered the first divorce ever at Rome might over time shed its complications, so as to become a plain dismissal for barrenness, the subsequent endowment of a plain dismissal with these subtleties would be difficult to explain. There is admittedly one consideration the other way. Both Dionysius – who brings in the census – and Valerius Maximus – with straightforward dismissal – mention that Ruga incurred lasting unpopularity. It is arguable that this would be more likely if he sent away a fine wife merely because he desired children than if he felt compelled by his oath. Still, even in the latter case, the adverse response is quite understandable. Over two thousand years before Freud, people sensed what lurks underneath so delicate a conscience.

The expression 'in order to seek children', or an equivalent, is frequent outside the census. Sometimes the duty element is noticeable, sometimes it is not – though even here it may be just below the surface.

It is not noticeable in Plautus, Ennius or Varro.[1] As one would expect, it is in a motion by a censor in

---

[1] Plautus, *The Pot of Gold* 2.1.27.148f. *liberis procreandis*, *The Captives* 4.2.109.888f. *liberorum quaerendorum causa*; Festus, *On the Meaning of Words* 258 *liberum quaesendum causa*, *liberorum sibi quaesendum gratia* (on the replacement of *causa* by *gratia*, loftier and less legalistic, see H. D. Jocelyn, *The Tragedies of Ennius*, 1967, p.277); Macrobius *Saturnalia* 1.16.18 *liberum quaerendorum causa.*

131 B.C., that all men should be compelled by law 'to take wives for the sake of producing children'.[1] The speech went under the title 'On the Need for More Progeny'.[2]

In a statute prepared, though not passed, under Caesar, the clause seems to signify merely entry into matrimony, without indicating an obligation. After his assassination, Suetonius informs us, a tribune revealed that the dictator had requested a law that was to be moved in his absence from Rome, so as to appear to be forced on him: he would be allowed 'to take to wife, in order to seek children, whomever and however many he wanted'[3] – that is to say, to contract a legitimate marriage with somebody like Cleopatra, an Egyptian, and to live in legitimate polygamy. Dio Cassius is significantly looser: he would be allowed 'to have intercourse with as many women as he wanted'.[4] This neglects *conubium* with an alien and, indeed, legitimacy, all-important for the status of any offspring. According to Dio, the statute was thought up by others, be it in order to flatter Caesar, be it in order to expose him to ridicule or hatred.

Some authorities hold that Caesar desired, or was

[1] Livy, *From the Foundation of the City*, Summaries 59 *liberorum creandorum causa*.
[2] Suetonius, *Augustus* 89.2 *de prole augenda*.
[3] Suetonius, *Julius* 52.3 *liberorum quaerendorum causa*; cp. Gellius, *Attic Nights* 16.7.3, quoting Laberius.
[4] Dio Cassius, *Roman History* 54.7.3 *syneinai*.

rumoured to desire, not a personal privilege but a general admission of polygamy, with a view to stemming the decrease in population.[1] We shall come back to his interest in this problem. If such was the tenor of the statute – and there are Greek precedents[2] – the phrase 'in order to seek children' certainly emphasizes a duty. On balance, however, the interpretation of the plan as in aid of his amours is preferable. For one thing, the grant of *conubium* to foreign women – strangely neglected by those who have commented – is highly suspicious. The idea of legalized polygamy or polyandry, incidentally, tickled the Romans: it is enough to recall the origin attributed by them (rightly or wrongly) to the surname Praetextatus, 'wearer of a boy's toga'.[3]

From Augustus's marriage legislation, the notion of duty distinctly attaches to the clause which, in fact, henceforth tends to figure in marriage documents, professing compliance with the state's demands. In the legislation itself it was laid down, for

[1] J.G.Heineccius, *Antiquitatum Romanarum Syntagma*, ed. C.F.Mühlenbruch (1841) p.135; T.Mommsen, *Römische Geschichte*, 9th ed. (1904) vol.3, p.591; L.Robinson, *Freedom of Speech in the Roman Republic* (1940) p.44; F.Schulz, *Classical Roman Law* (1951) p.112; M.Kaser, *Das römische Privatrecht*, pt.1 (1955) p.269.
[2] Diogenes Laertius, *Lives of the Philosophers 2* (Socrates) 26; Athenaeus, *Deipnosophists* 13.2.556a; cp. Gellius, *Attic Nights* 15.20.6.
[3] Gellius, *Attic Nights* 1.23; Macrobius, *Saturnalia* 1.6.18ff; cp. Polybius, *Histories* 3.20.3.

example, that if a husband leaves something to his wife on condition that she does not remarry, she nevertheless has a claim on swearing that she re-marries 'in order to produce offspring'.[1] The docu-mentary evidence stretches from papyri of the first century A.D., where a father 'gives away his virgin daughter in accordance with the *lex Julia* concerning the marriage of the classes, in order to produce children',[2] to Augustine, who half a dozen times at least adduces the matrimonial tablets stipulating this purpose.[3] From Tacitus we hear that even the docu-ment drawn up at the outrageous wedding of Messalina, Claudius's Empress, and Silius contained the words 'in order to have children'.[4] The verb *suscipere* here used can signify not only 'to beget' or 'to give birth to' but also 'to acknowledge as one's own'; maybe it seemed appropriate because Silius promised Messalina to adopt her son from Claudius, Britan-nicus.

The *lex Julia* was not the only Augustan statute employing the phrase. The *lex Julia Norbana* provided

[1] Justinian's *Code* 6.40.2 pr. *procreandae subolis gratia, Novellae* 22.43 *paidon heneka*; cp. *Digest* 35.1.64.1, Terentius Clemens V ad legem Juliam et Papiam.

[2] *PSI* (Pubblicazioni della Società per la Ricerca dei Papiri Greci e Latini in Egitto) 6.730, *Pap. Mich.* (Papyri Michigan) 508 *liberorum procreandorum causa*. See R. Astolfi, *La Lex Julia et Papia* (1970) pp.65f.

[3] *The City of God* 14.18, *Sermons* 9.11.18, 51.13.22, 278.9.9, 292.3 *liberorum procreandorum causa*.

[4] Tacitus, *Annals* 11.27 *liberorum suscipiendorum causa*.

that a Junian Latin who married a Roman or Latin woman, before citizens witnessing 'his taking a wife in order to seek children', might acquire citizenship on having a child one year old:[1] reward for dutiful conduct. A second-century papyrus, where a soldier attests the birth of a son to him, speaks of the *lex Aelia Sentia* and the *lex Papia Poppaea* as 'concerning the producing of children'.[2] As a judge, Augustus debarred a husband from keeping the dowry his deceased wife had given him, on the ground that they had not joined 'for the sake of producing children':[3] she had married him when they were both of advanced age, in order to deprive her sons from a previous marriage of her property. Horace, fervent supporter of the Emperor's policy, of course has duty in mind when he censures those 'who seek money and, for the producing of children, a rich wife'.[4] Even while they satisfy the laws, their heart is not, as it ought to be, in 'seeking children': it is in 'seeking wealth'.

The tracing of this expression through the better part of a millennium has taken us ahead of our story and we must return to the Republic. Towards the end of the fifth century B.C., we saw, the censors levied an old bachelors' fine. The Punic wars in the third

[1] Ulpian, *Regulae* 3.3 *liberorum quaerendorum causa*.
[2] *Pap. Mich.* 7.436 *de filiis procreandis*. See R. Astolfi, op. cit., p.67f.
[3] Valerius Maximus, *Memorable Deeds and Sayings* 7.7.4 *creandorum liberorum causa*.
[4] Horace, *Epistles* 1.2.44 *pueris creandis*.

century were costly in lives of citizens; and in the refined, leading circles, replacement was slow. Simultaneously, the slave and foreign elements expanded at a stupendous rate. When we consider, in addition, that a wave of Hellenistic ethos swept in just then, it is no wonder that the concept of reproduction as a duty gained ground. To illustrate the kind of transmission to be reckoned with: Polybius, in his chapter on the conflict between Rome and Macedonia, deplores the depopulation of Greece and the growing aversion of people to the burden of marriage and children; and he recommends legislation.[1] Doubtless he was acquainted with a recent effort by Philip v of Macedonia.[2] The point here relevant is his friendship with Aemilius Paulus and his son, the younger Scipio Africanus.

For a long time, it remained the task of the censors to bring to bear what pressure the government deemed advisable. In 131 B.C., as already mentioned, one of them called for far-reaching legal measures.[3] He, too, knew about Philip: it was Q. Caecilius Metellus, surnamed Macedonicus because of his subjugation of Macedonia, forty years or so after Philip's death. Livy says that the proposal was 'to force all'[4] – the same expression that he uses in writing about

[1] Polybius, *Histories* 36.17.5ff., alternatively numbered 37.4.1ff. or 37.9.1ff.
[2] Livy, *From the Foundation of the City* 39.24.3.
[3] Livy, *From the Foundation of the City*, Summaries 59; Suetonius, *Augustus* 89.2.   [4] *Cogere omnes.*

Philip. Gellius tells us that Macedonius's nephew, when censor in 102 B.C., in an address 'On the Need for Matrimony', exhorted the male citizens for the sake of the continued existence of the state to forgo the superior attractions of bachelorhood for marriage and procreation.[1] Or, as Gellius's teacher in rhetoric summed it up: 'The state cannot be sound without numerous marriages'. All good Greek stuff. It is widely held that Gellius errs and there was only one speech, by the uncle. This is far from proved[2] and, even if it were, would not affect the development as a whole.

Cicero's constitution also puts the censors in charge: 'they shall prohibit men from being celibate'.[3] The language suggests that they are to go beyond sermonizing and put teeth into their edict. Possibly, he gives them more to do than has been realized. The preceding ordinance is commonly translated 'they shall enrol recruits for the cavalry and rank'.[4] *Proles*, 'offspring', is thus credited with a transferred sense met nowhere else.[5] Considering the artificial style of

[1] Gellius, *Attic Nights* 1.6 *de ducendis uxoribus*.
[2] See J. C. Rolfe, *The Attic Nights of Aulus Gellius* (Loeb Classical Library) vol.1 (1927) pp.30f.
[3] Cicero, *On the Laws* 3.3.7 *caelibes esse prohibunto*.
[4] See C. W. Keyes, *Cicero, de Re Publica, de Legibus* (Loeb Classical Library) (1928) p.45. G. De Plinval, *Cicéron, Traité des Lois* (1959) p.84, has: *qu'ils répartissent les jeunes classes entre cavaliers et piétons*.
[5] Virgil, *Aeneid* 10.429, cited in C. T. Lewis and C. Short, *A Latin Dictionary* (repr. 1969) p.1463, is no parallel.

his laws,[1] this is defensible. Maybe, however, we should render literally: 'they shall determine the progeny for the higher and lower orders'. They are to lay down, that is, how many children are due from a couple according as they belong to one class or another, or two different classes. (If *equites peditesque* simply signifies 'the entire people',[2] he may be thinking of numbers only: 'they shall fix the progeny for the citizen body'.) After all, this work avowedly imitates Plato.[3]

According to the sources, Caesar was proclaimed not only dictator but also *praefectus morum*, a kind of super-censor.[4] Mommsen maintains that there was no room for the latter honour since all its rights and duties were covered by the former. Hardly conclusive – but it does not matter: he agrees that Caesar exercised to the full a censor's functions.[5] Actually, already on first obtaining the consulate, when he had the territory of Capua distributed, he gave preference to the father of three or more children. Later, alarmed by the censuses which revealed the tremendous cost

[1] Cicero, *On the Laws* 2.7.18.
[2] cp. Livy, *From the Foundation of the City* 1.44.1, quoted by C.T.Lewis and C.Short, op. cit., p.1326.
[3] Cicero, *On the Laws* 1.15.5.
[4] Cicero, *To his Friends* 9.15.5; Suetonius, *Julius* 76.1; Dio Cassius, *Roman History* 43.14.4, 25.2, 44.5.3.
[5] See T.Mommsen, *Römisches Staatsrecht*, vol.2, pt.1, 3rd ed. (1887) pp.705f., *Römische Geschichte* vol.3, 9th ed. (1904) pp.211, 533, 538.

of the civil war, he offered prizes for large families.[1]

Throughout those centuries, however, side by side with advocacy of propagation, we find advocacy of Stoic abstemiousness. The resultant ideal was that you should indeed marry and produce children but have no sex for fun. The younger Cato had touched no woman before he married.[2] Lucan sings of him: 'For him, this is the greatest benefit of Venus: offspring. To aid the city he is a father, and to aid the city a husband'.[3] (In modern editions, 'greatest' is pedantically emended into 'only'.[4]) Other Platonic conceits were current, and the same Cato's life offers an illustration regarding community of wives and children.[5] The orator Hortensius asked him for the

---

[1] Suetonius, *Julius* 20.3; Appian, *Civil Wars* 2.2.10, 2.15.102; Dio Cassius, *Roman History* 38.7.3, 25.2.

[2] Plutarch, *The Younger Cato* 7.1.   [3] Lucan, *Pharsalia* 2.387f.

[4] R. Bentley started it; and A. E. Housman supplied a brilliant conjecture of how *unicus* became *maximus* (*Lucani Belli Civilis Libri Decem*, 1927, pp.44f.). It reminds me of a note by Wilfred Knox of 6 June 1942. He had published an article (*Harvard Theological Review*, vol.35, 1942, pp.13ff.) maintaining that the Gospel of Mark once had an ending which is no longer extant; and I had asked him, stupidly, how he thought it disappeared. He wrote: 'Of course if you are going to ask why the ending is lost, my theory is that in the *paroxysmos* of Acts 15.39 St Paul grabbed the copy of Mark off the table, and St Barnabas, in attempting to grab it back, got the ending and went off with it to Cyprus. After all, these holy men were only human!' The difference is that Knox was joking.

[5] Plutarch, *The Younger Cato* 25, 52.3ff.; Plato, *Republic* 5.1.449Cff. 7.457Cff., 9.460Bff.; cp. Isaeus, *On the Estate of Menecles*.

hand of his daughter, married at the time to Cal-
purnius Bibulus, to whom she had borne two sons. He
submitted that, according to natural morality, a
young, excellent woman ought neither to lie fallow
nor impoverish a husband by too many children. He
himself, it may be remarked, was a widower in his
late fifties with several children, but very rich. The
state, his argument went on, would gain in strength
by the kind of alliance emerging if both Bibulus and
he had offspring from Cato's daughter. If Bibulus was
wrapped up in her, he would give her back for re-
marriage after she had done her job – which would
make the bond between all of them even closer. Cato
declined this proposal but agreed to let him marry his
wife who had given him enough children; a new one
was indeed on the way just then. After Hortensius's
death he remarried her, and the orator's estate came
to him. What deserves notice is the taking over from
the Greek model of such details as the emphasis on
genetic desirability and economic factors: quantity is
not the only consideration. Caesar, it is true, in his
Anticato, shows little belief in the high-minded moti-
vation of the parties.

Up to the end of the Republic, whatever the moral
trend, no general legal disabilities befell a person who
stayed single. Augustus's famous laws changed this.[1]

[1] The literature is enormous. For a modern viewpoint, see
R.I.Frank, 'Augustus's Legislation on Marriage and Children',
in *California Studies in Classical Antiquity*, vol.8 (1975) pp.41ff.

Besides rewarding prolific parents, they penalized men between twenty-five and sixty and women between twenty and fifty if unmarried or married but childless.[1] He was fully conscious of strengthening a traditional line: in recommending his plan, he read to the senate the speech of Macedonicus of some hundred-and-twenty years before.[2] The major considerations may indeed come down (no matter through what channels) right from the early confrontation of Hellas and Persia. To go by Dio, the Emperor explained that, unless his policy was carried out, 'the Greeks or even the barbarians' would take over.[3] In the era of Darius and Xerxes, the Greeks had feared the barbarians. Now, for the Romans, the Greeks – in the wider sense – were the danger, but the barbarians are still mentioned. Admittedly, new barbarians were at the gate, and from Tacitus it is evident that their reproductive capacity was noticed with alarm.[4] It is doubtful, however, whether they would appear in the argument but for their routine standing in it. At any rate, the proportion of the legislation due (directly or via intermediaries) to Greek philosophy and statecraft is striking. As in Plato, the rewards and penalties are partly economic,

[1] Dio Cassius, *Roman History* 53.13.2, 54.16.1, 55.2.6, 56.10; Ulpian, *Regulae* 13ff.
[2] Livy, *From the Foundation of the City*, Summaries 59; Suetonius, *Augustus* 89.2.
[3] Dio Cassius, *Roman History* 56.7.5.
[4] Tacitus, *Histories* 5.5, *Germany* 19.

partly status-directed. As in Plato – and contrary to good Roman sentiment – a widow with not yet enough children is to remarry. As in Aristotle, three and four children are standard figures.

There are differences. One is that women no less than men come under these legal regulations: by this time they needed the same prodding. Another is subtler, illustrating the fact that similar measures may have very dissimilar effect, when applied in changed circumstances. The kind of sanction that, in an ancient Greek city, affected high and low among the free part of the population, at the Rome of Augustus would be meaningful solely to the former. (Noticed by Pliny.[1]) If you are unmarried, you may receive inheritances and bequests only from certain close relations such as parents; and at the ritual assumption of the consulate your married colleague takes precedence of you. A freeborn woman who has borne three children or a freedwoman who has borne four is rid of her guardian, hence able without his authority to convey by formal act land, slaves and cattle or to appoint a *cognitor* as well as a *procurator*.[2] Few of those who slept under the bridges of the Tiber can have been moved by these rules. It is commonly held that

Pliny, *Panegyric* 26.5.

[2] 'Consuls' Gellius, *Attic Nights* 2.15.4ff., *Vatican Fragments* 197, Ulpian de officio praetoris tutelaris; 'guardianship' Gaius, *Institutes* 3.44, Ulpian, *Regulae* 29.3, Paul, *Sentences* 4.9.1ff.

the legislation accomplished nothing: 'By granting petty honours . . . the Roman population could not possibly be saved. Substantial . . . support to parents blessed with large families might have been effective'. Or again: 'It was . . . a terrible blunder of Augustus to prohibit soldiers of the rank and file from marrying . . . As the length of service was very long a particularly vigorous part of the Roman population was debarred from marrying for the best part of its life'.[1] This, however, is to look at the matter from the angle of early twentieth-century liberalism. Very likely, Augustus knew, and got, what he wanted; for one thing, the rabble proliferated anyhow. In passing: when he required more children from people domiciled elsewhere than from residents of the capital, and again, more from a freedwoman than from a freeborn woman, what may have played a part, besides population-political ends and fairness to patrons, is the feeling that for simpler folks, and especially for women of lowly origin, children and child-bearing are less of a burden than for their betters.

It is not necessary to pursue the Roman side beyond this point. The venerable notions keep being carried on. Musonius dwells on the patriotic aspect of parenthood. Pliny eulogizes Trajan for ensuring the future of the empire by his bounties to the poor of Rome and their little ones. Lucan, as already mentioned, looks

[1] See F. Schulz, *Classical Roman Law* (1951) pp.108, 113.

down even on wedded love not geared towards procreation, and so does Plutarch; and extremists
recommend absolute purity.[1]

3) *Judaism and Early Christianity* (

IT IS IN THE ERA of Augustus that the duty of
procreation made its way into Judaism. Pseudo-
Phocylides declaims against letting your name perish;
and you ought to repay nature for what you have
received.[2] Philo is fundamentally hostile to the flesh.
None the less the law of nature bids man reproduce.
Hence you should marry – but for this purpose only:
even between spouses intercourse for mere pleasure is
base.[3] For Josephus, the law approves exclusively the
natural union of husband and wife, and even this for
the sake of progeny only. He knows a dissident
branch of Essenes who, unlike the majority, deem the
continuance of the race so important that they feel
obliged to marry; though as soon as a wife is pregnant,
the husband abstains from further intimacy.[4] The
idea of procreation as a duty must have been around

[1] Musonius, *Reliquiae* ed. O. Hense (1905) p.69; Pliny,
Panegyric 25ff.; Lucan, *Pharsalia* 2.387f.; Plutarch, *On Affection
for Offspring* 2 (*Moralia* 493Ef.); Plotinus, *Enneads* 1.6.6.
[2] Pseudo-Phocylides, *Poem of Admonition* 175f.
[3] Philo, *The Worse attacks the Better* 27.102, *Abraham* 26.135ff.,
Joseph 9.43f., *Moses* 1.6.28, *Special Laws* 3.6.32ff., 20.113,
Questions on Genesis 1.27, 4.86.
[4] Josephus, *Against Apion* 2.24.199, *Jewish War* 2.8.13.160f.

for a good while for such a splinter-group to come into being – which corroborates the date given above.

While these testimonies have a distinctly Hellenistic-philosophical flavour, the earliest, more legalistic Rabbinic ones – quoting the Schools of Hillel and Shammai – extend back into the same period.[1] Still, from the silence of the New Testament, despite plenty of opportunity for speaking out,[2] it looks as if the new obligation attained full recognition only towards the end of the first century A.D.

Both Philo and the Rabbis of the first two centuries hold that the husband of a barren woman ought to divorce her, in order to marry another. Puzzling, since polygamy was licit at the time, so he could take an additional wife. Doubly puzzling, in view of the respectable Scriptural precedents for the latter course.[3] R. Yaron suggests that we have to do with a borrowing from non-Jewish, monogamous society.[4] This is correct. But why did it happen? The answer is that the duty to procreate was adopted together with the machinery of compliance. Indeed, the appearance of the latter, totally incongruous within the Jewish system, places beyond doubt the alien provenance of the former.

[1] *Mishnah Yebamoth 6.6.*
[2] Matthew 19.3ff., 1 Corinthians 7.
[3] Genesis 16.1ff., 30.3ff.
[4] In a piece that was to form part of a joint volume by D. Daube and R. Yaron. Delays on the part of the sponsors have led to the abandonment of the plan.

It has been argued that divorce was recommended because most Jews then in fact lived monogamously. But the polygamous way out is not contemplated even in the most heartbreaking circumstances. A loving couple who had to part because of the wife's barrenness were advised by Rabbi Simeon ben Johai to have a divorce banquet. (A very Californian idea.) Having drunk freely, the husband told her to take with her whatever she liked best in his home; and when he was asleep, she had her servants carry him himself to her father's house. Of course, she now conceived and all was well.[1] Surely, where polygamy is O.K., even though not common, the whole plot makes no sense. This story also shows that the Rabbinic statements cannot be explained as meant for people too poor to afford polygamy. These two had the wherewithal for a huge festivity and they had servants, too. It is highly significant that from the third century on the alternative of marrying a second wife in addition does figure:[2] the foreign institution has been assimilated.

The import was the result of a combination of factors. Well before Augustus, the Jewish leadership must have paid attention to pagan thought and action in the field of population policy. The communities of the dispersion, in constant danger of being engulfed,

[1] *Song of Songs Rabba* on 1.4. See Stith Thompson, *Motif-Index of Folk-Literature*, vol.4, J–K (1957) p.124.
[2] *Babylonian Yebamoth* 65af.

would be the first to do so. But urbanisation and
allied phenomena imperilled replenishment in Pale-
stine also. Then came the Augustan decrees and the
debates surrounding them, which fascinated the entire
realm – not only jurists but the educated public at
large.[1] Finally, the ruinous war with Rome of 66–70 –
let alone the rebellion under Hadrian – rendered the
situation desperate.[2] (Judah ben Ilai, who helped steer
the nation through the Hadrianic persecution, likened
one who knowingly married a sterile woman to the
visitor of a harlot.[3]) Which of the Talmudic pro-
nouncements are due to general Hellenistic inspira-
tion, which to the laws of Augustus in particular and
which to internal evolution may be left open.

Three contrasts between the Rabbis and Augustus
may be noted. The Rabbinic obligation was of a
religious nature, and hence fell on high and low
equally. Augustus employed financial and civic
inducements and deterrents. The Rabbis confined
themselves to something akin to the latter: a scholar,
for example, who neglected the duty might find it
difficult to achieve ordination.[4] (Possibly this played

---

[1] Horace, *Odes* 4.5.21ff.; Ovid, *Fasti* 2.139f.; Martial,
Epigrams 6.7, 21. Trials under the *lex Julia de adulteriis* are
reported by Josephus, *Jewish Antiquities* 18.3.4.65ff.
[2] *Tosephta Sotah* 15.10, *Babylonian Baba Bathra* 60b.
[3] *Mishnah Yebamoth* 6.5.
[4] *Babylonian Qiddushin* 29b; see D. Daube, *Medical and Genetic
Ethics*, p.10.

a part in the case of Simeon ben Azzai. His apology, incidentally, that his soul was bound up with the Torah, is reminiscent of philosophical argumentation.[1]) Most striking is the Rabbinic restriction of the duty to males, with interesting consequences: for instance, it would be sinful for a childless man to take a sterilizing drug, but not for a childless woman. A minority combated this *privilegium odiosum*; indeed, praise was bestowed on the daughters of Lot for sleeping with him when it seemed that he was the only male left alive and that there was no other way to repopulate the world. It would lead too far afield here to pursue the controversy.[2] It will be noticed that in all the three points of divergence from Rome, the Rabbis seem nearer some Greek doctrines.

The defence of Lot's daughters shews what one would expect: once procreation was looked on as a primeval commandment, it became part of the small, basic code binding not only on Jews but on all mankind. (Corresponding to the Greek law of nature.[3]) It is none the less absent from all *ex professo* discussions of that code in Talmud and Midrash – let alone the

---

[1] *Tosephta Qiddushin* 3.9, *Yebamoth* 8.4; Epictetus, *Discourses* 3.22.69.
[2] 'Johanan's thesis' *Mishnah Yebamoth* 6.6, *Genesis Rabba* on 1.28; 'sterilization' *Babylonian Shabbath* 111a; 'Lot' Genesis 19.30ff., *Babylonian Horayoth* 10b. More fully explored by David Daube, 'Johanan ben Beroqa and Women's Rights', in a forthcoming volume in memory of W. Fischel.
[3] cp. Philo, *Rewards and Punishments* 18.108.

Book of Jubilees.[1] Here is yet another sign of its relatively late arrival.

In the Christian sources, as in the Rabbinic ones, reproduction is described as laudable from the second century on: Justin Martyr, Athenagoras, Clement of Alexandria come to mind.[2] It is, however, a *pis aller*; if you cannot do without sex, marriage for the sake of procreation is the proper course. Abstention is superior. No doubt adherence to the New Testament ideal[3] was facilitated by the fact that the catastrophe of A.D. 70 hit the new group less severely; indeed, its membership increased at a rapid pace. This influx of heathens has a bearing on another deviation from the dominant Rabbinic view: the Church Fathers impose the duty on females as well as males. While the nature of marital union proclaimed by Jesus is plainly the chief cause, a subsidiary one may well reside in the position of gentile women, more independent and less keen on childbearing than their Jewish sisters.

Sirach in the early second century B.C. can still advise that it is better to have no children than wicked ones. According to a Rabbinic exposition of

[1] *Tosephta Abodah Zarah* 8.4ff., *Babylonian Yoma* 67b, *Sanhedrin* 56bff., *Hullin* 92a, *Siphra* on Leviticus 18.4, *Deuteronomy Rabba* on 4.41, Jubilees 7.20ff.
[2] Justin, *Apology for Christians* 1.29; Athenagoras, *Legation on behalf of Christians* 33; Clement of Alexandria, *Stromata* 2.23.140.1. See J. T. Noonan, op. cit., pp.30ff.
[3] For the jurisprudential background, see D. Daube, *Journal of Jewish Studies* 10 (1959) p.11.

around A.D. 300, King Hezekiah's near-fatal illness recorded in the Bible befell him because, having been informed by the holy spirit that any issue of his would be godless, he refrained from marriage.[1] Such a legend would be inconceivable in the Church Fathers.

6

In conclusion, let us glance at some of the perennial features in this domain. Traditionally, France looks with dread at the extra millions of Germany, Germany at those of Russia, Russia at those of China. But the danger may come from within the borders: in present-day Britain, the dominant minority is increasingly troubled by the prospect of being outnumbered to a point where it might be overthrown. One way of handling the problem is to do better oneself: the treasury may subsidize large families, or large families of the right type, the president may send a con-gratulatory telegram on a fifth child. Another is to interfere with the rival, be it violently – waging war or genocide – or peacefully – by economic pressure, encouragement of birthcontrol (certain methods of which, to be sure, are not so gentle), immigration laws. The Egyptians of the Bible feared lest the Israelite settlers 'should multiply and when there falls out any war, join our enemies'. So here there is a

[1] Ecclesiasticus 16.1ff., *Babylonian Berakoth* 10a; see D. Daube, *Medical and Genetic Ethics*, pp.8ff.

combination – often repeated in history – of threat from inside and threat from outside. The king ended by opting for violence, ordering the midwives to kill any newborn Hebrew male.[1]

They disobeyed and, when questioned, explained that the Hebrew women gave birth so easily – maybe the word used at this point likens them to animals[2] – that by the time the midwife arrived the baby was already fully with the family. As remarked above, the assumption that the females in the lower strata have less difficulty about birth is common – one reason being that there is some truth in it. What should be added is that proliferation is apt to evoke very different reactions according as it takes place among your own set or among the enemy. In the former case, it is virtuous, in the latter you look down on the rabble that breeds like mice or rabbits.

On a more general level – this address has presented one of numerous instances of a blessing turning into a duty, moral or legal. One could almost write a history of civilisation around this theme. Wealth, it is said, was made into a moral obligation by Calvinism. Most Western societies have compulsory education, many have compulsory savings for old age. Sanitary plumbing is so strictly enforced in the States that Governor Brown has a tough job trying to get things

[1] Exodus 1.10ff.
[2] Exodus 1.19, *Exodus Rabba* 1 ad loc; see D. Daube, *Civil Disobedience in Antiquity* (1972) p.7.

relaxed a little for a few cabins in the woods. Life itself has undergone this transformation. In Scripture, it is a blessing: 'that your days may be long upon the land which the Lord gives you'.[1] Ordinarily it is cherished, but if I do not like it I am free to renounce it. Later on it became a duty; not seldom a legal one, suicide constituting a felony. What chiefly accounts for this trend is that the goods a person feels to be blessings – or at least those publicly acknowledged as such – are as a rule useful to the common weal – or at least to whoever sets the tone. Accordingly, the shift towards duty occurs when two conditions coincide: first, people are less eager than official interest requires, and secondly, it is possible to do something about it.

To be sure, the pendulum can swing to the opposite side again. Several countries have recently de-criminalized suicide, though, even now, it is not nice. The very duty to reproduce is being eroded every-where to a remarkable extent. On the other hand, there are not a few blessings on the verge of changing into moral oughts or legal musts. Examples from America would be medical check-ups, multiple orgasm and the vote.

[1] Exodus 20.12.